Women Who Rock

TAYLOR Swift

GAIL TERP

BLACK RABBIT BOOKS

Bolt is published by Black Rabbit Books
P.O. Box 227, Mankato, Minnesota, 56002.
www.blackrabbitbooks.com

Design and Production by Michael Sellner
Photo Research by Rhonda Milbrett

Library of Congress Control Number: 2015954911

HC ISBN: 978-1-68072-069-3 PB ISBN: 978-1-68072-319-9

Printed in the United States

Web addresses included in this book were working and appropriate at the time of publication. The publisher is not responsible for broken or changed links.

Image Credits

Corbis: Andrew Orth /Retna Ltd., 11, 12; Daniel DeSlover/ZUMA Press, 20–21; Getty: Brian Rasic, 24; Dimitrios Kambouris/LP5, 4–5; Jesse D. Garrabrant, 8 (right); John Shearer/LP5, 6–7; Michael Loccisano, 23; Michael Stewart, Cover; Shirlaine Forrest, 18 (top); Newscom: David Morley/Splash News, 15; Shutterstock: DFree, 8–9; Everett Collection, 9 (right), 17; FashionStock.com, Back Cover, 1, 27; i4lcocl2, 9 (bottom); JStone, 32; lem, 3, 28–29; SoleilC, 10–11, 31; Wikimedia: 18 (bottom)

Every effort has been made to contact copyright holders for material reproduced in this book. Any omissions will be rectified in subsequent printings if notice is given to the publisher.

Contents

CHAPTER 1

Secret Sessions

The private messages went out to a few Taylor Swift fans. The messages told them where to meet for a special opportunity. But they didn't give more details. On the day of the event, a bus drove the fans to a house. They soon realized it was Swift's house. But they didn't know why they were there.

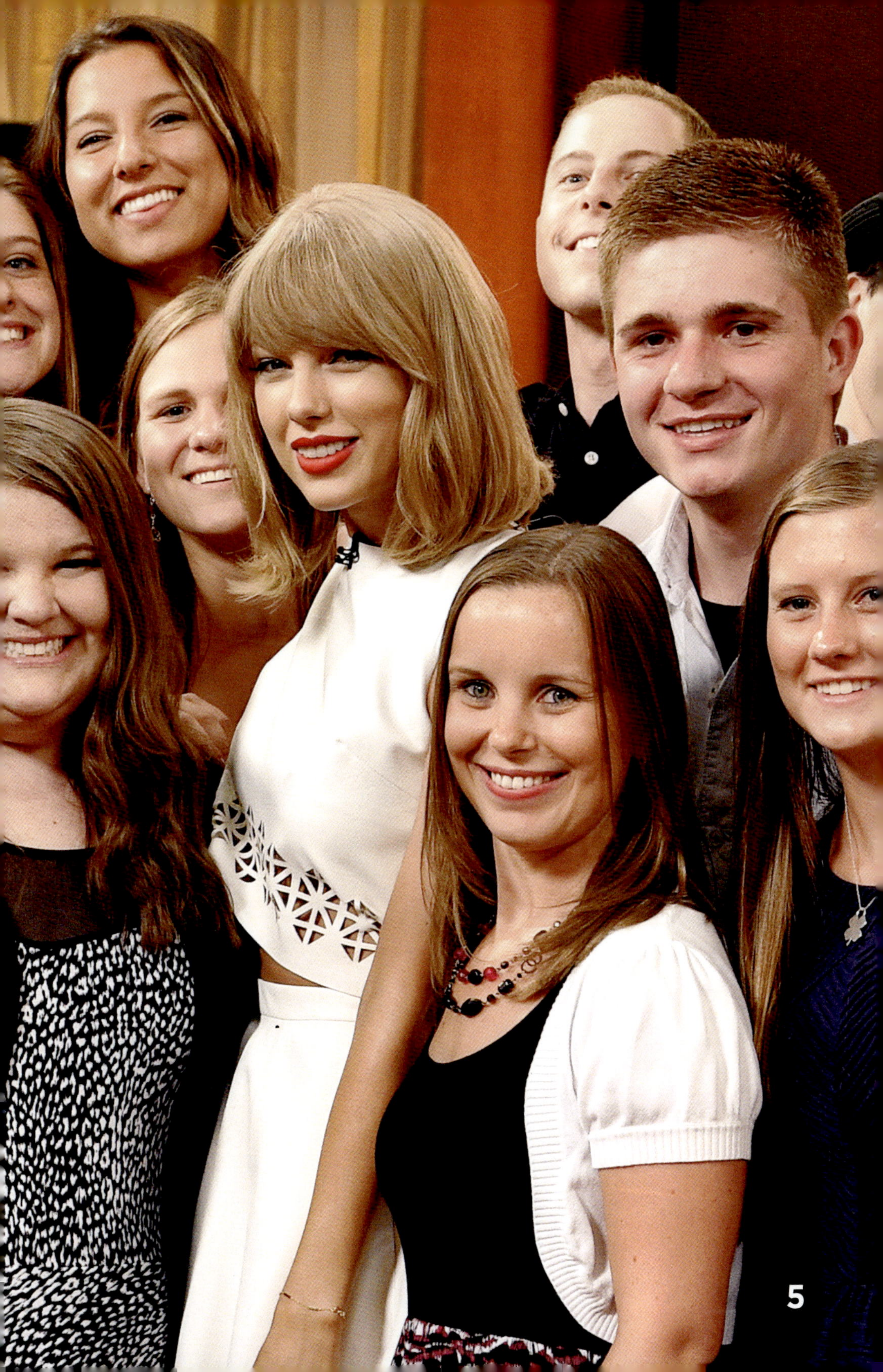

Superstar

The fans soon learned what was going on. Swift walked in. The fans screamed in delight. She had planned this surprise for months. Her new CD, *1989*, had not yet come out. She wanted her top fans to hear it first.

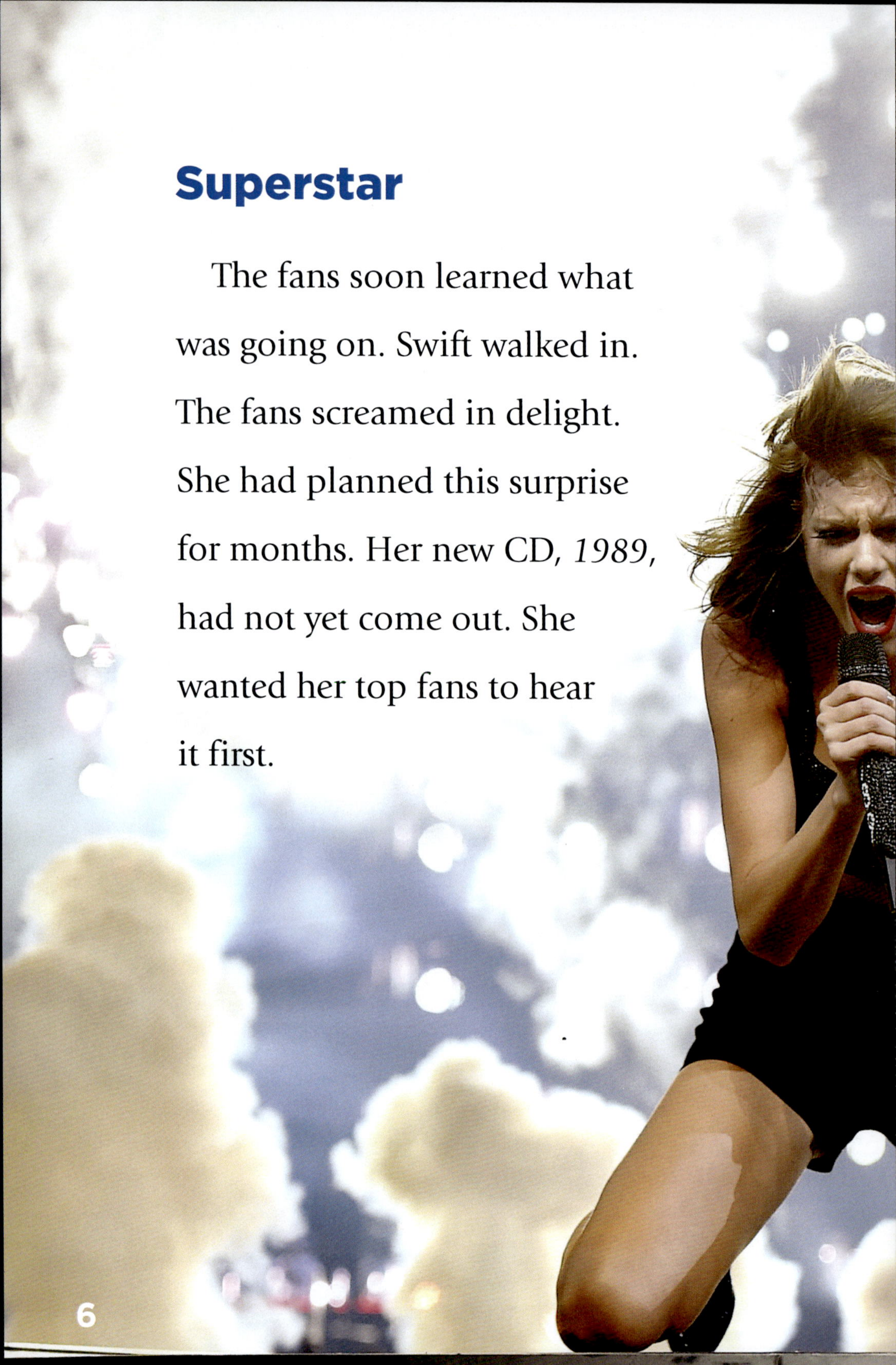

Taylor Swift is a superstar. She's won many **Grammy** awards. Her concerts sell out. And yet she still invited fans to her home. Many say her kindness is a big reason for her success.

Swift had five secret listening parties.

Fun Facts

6'

5'

4'

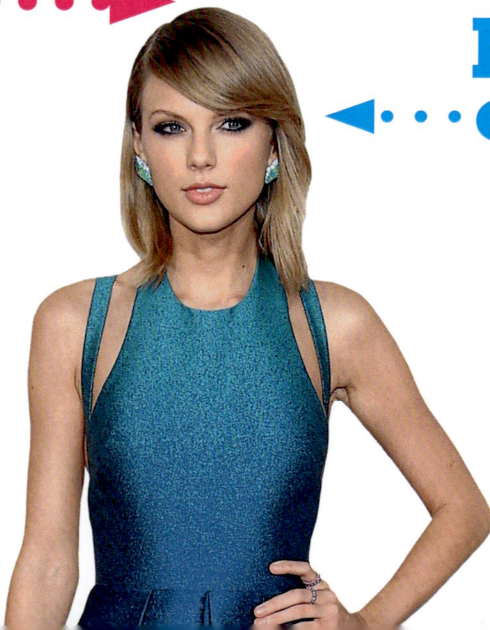

blue eyes

PLAYS

GUITAR
BANJO
PIANO
UKULELE

age 12

WROTE HER FIRST SONG

5 feet
10 inches
(1.8 m) tall

NAMED AFTER SINGER
JAMES TAYLOR

GREW UP ON
A CHRISTMAS
TREE FARM

OWNS A JET

CHAPTER 2

Early Years

Swift was born December 13, 1989. She and her family lived in Pennsylvania. When she was young, she loved to ride horses.

By age 9, Swift knew she also loved to sing. She acted in **musicals**. When she was 11, she won a singing contest. She started writing songs too. Music was definitely her talent.

Country Music

At age 12, Swift learned to play guitar. She practiced for hours each day. She played and sang country music. When she was 14, Swift and her family moved to Nashville, Tennessee. Her parents knew she should be there. It's the center of country music.

First Album

Swift's first big break came soon after her move. Scott Borchetta heard her singing in a café. Borchetta records and sells music. He asked Swift to work with him. Swift's first album, *Taylor Swift*, came out in 2006. It sold more than 5 million copies. Swift was only 16 years old.

Swift's fans are called Swifties.

Taylor

CHAPTER 3

Making It Big

Swift didn't slow down after her first album. Her next album was *Fearless*. It was the 2009 top seller in the United States. *Speak Now* came out in 2010. That album sold more than 1 million copies in the first week. Swift released *Red* in 2012. In about two months, it was the year's second top seller.

4,410,000
3,110,000
1,620,000
1,460,000
1,340,000
1,000,000
1,500,000
2,000,000
2,500,000
3,000,000
3,500,000
4,000,000
4,500,000

T.S. 1989

The Switch

Two years after *Red, 1989* hit stores. The songs on this album weren't like Swift's other songs. Her songs before had been country music. *1989* was a **pop** album. This switch in style didn't hurt Swift's success. The album was the 2014 top seller in the United States.

Why did she name it that?

Swift named her album *1989* for the year she was born.

COMPARING STARS

Popular musicians make a lot of money. See how Swift compares to other popular acts.

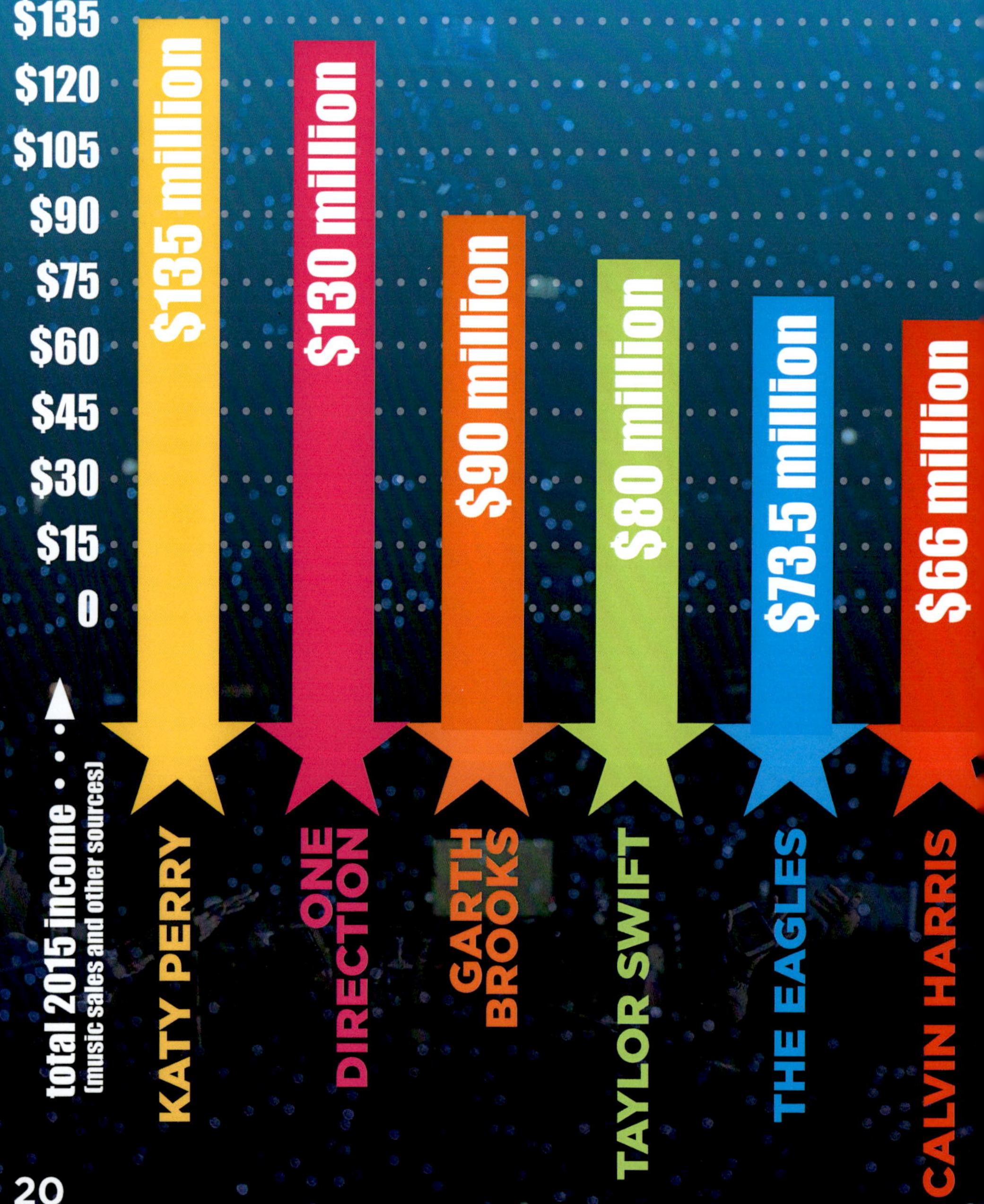

JUSTIN TIMBERLAKE
$63.5 million
DIDDY
$60 million
FLEETWOOD MAC
$59.5 million
LADY GAGA
$59 million
THE ROLLING STONES
$57.5 million
ED SHEERAN
$57 million

CHAPTER 4

Swift Today

Swift's fame has made her a powerful person. In 2015, Apple Music started a new **streaming** plan. It let customers stream free for three months. Apple refused to pay musicians for their songs during those three months. Swift fought back. She said she would not let her *1989* album stream. Apple quickly changed its rules. It now pays musicians during the free months.

Some of Swift's Donations

$15,000
family hurt in car crash

$50,000
fan with cancer

Generous Swift

Unlike most stars, Swift talks with her fans a lot. She messages them on **social media**. She visits them when they are sick. She sends them presents. She even gives them advice online. Swift is also **generous** with her money.

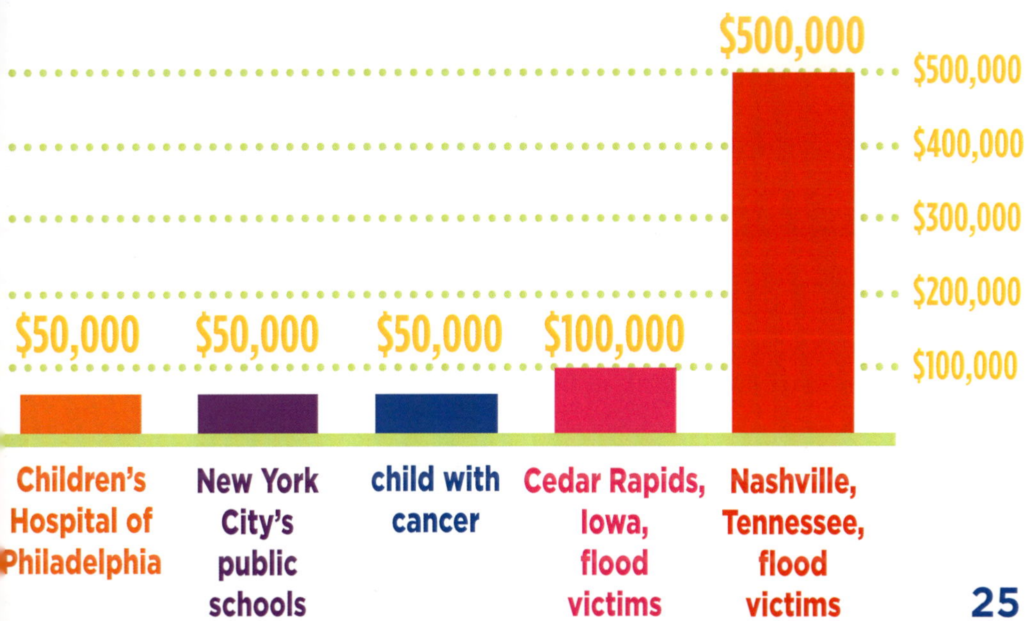

In the Spotlight

Fans say Swift is one of the best musicians ever. Other people disagree. They say her voice is thin and her songs are silly. But no one can doubt she has star power. And she's likely to stay in the spotlight for years to come.

TIMELINE

1989 born in Pennsylvania

2003 moves to Nashville

2004

2005

2006 releases first album, *Taylor Swift*

2007

releases *Fearless*

2008

2009

wins four awards at the Country Music Awards

2010

releases *Speak Now*

wins four Grammy awards

2011

2012

releases *Red*

2013

2014

releases *1989*

2015

uses star power to make Apple Music pay musicians fairly

generous (JEN-ur-us)—freely giving or sharing

Grammy (GRAM-ee)—an award given for outstanding work in recorded music

musical (MYU-zi-kuhl)—a play or movie that tells a story with songs and often dancing

pop (PAHP)—a style of music with a strong beat and simple tunes

social media (SO-shul ME-de-uh)—forms of electronic communication through which users create online communities to share content

streaming (STREEM-ing)—playing continuously as data is sent to a computer over the Internet

ukulele (yoo-kuh-LAY-lee)—a musical instrument that is like a small guitar

BOOKS

Cupp, Tonya. *Taylor Swift.* Celebrity Entrepreneurs. New York: Cavendish Square Publishing, 2015.

Frisch, Aaron. *Taylor Swift.* The Big Time. Mankato, MN: Creative Education, 2013.

Heatley, Michael. *Taylor Swift: Country Music's American Sweetheart.* Broomall, PA: Mason Crest, 2015.

WEBSITES

Taylor Swift
taylorswift.com

Taylor Swift
www.mtv.com/artists/taylor-swift/

Taylor Swift Q & A
www.timeforkids.com/photos-video/video/taylor-swift-qa-200061

INDEX